The St

Written by Tina Shaw
Illustrated by Jono Smith

PEARSON

Amy and Josh were brother and sister, but they couldn't have been more different. Amy loved being the centre of attention, while Josh preferred to hide in corners. You could hear Amy coming, but Josh crept around like a mouse. Amy talked and sang and laughed at the top of her voice, while Josh, when he did speak – which wasn't all that often – had a very quiet voice. Josh was so quiet, in fact, that people often forgot he was in the room. Amy, on the other hand, simply wouldn't let anybody forget *she* was around.

So, when Amy got a part in the school production, the family wasn't surprised.

"I'm going to be a stick insect," she announced exuberantly during dinner. "I get to do the stick insect dance all by myself! *And* I'm the very first one on!" Mum and Dad smiled. That was so like Amy. "And Josh is going to make my costume," she added smugly.

Everybody looked at Josh, who just sat there nodding. Josh was good with his hands and often spent hours in the garage working on complicated and elaborate projects. A stick insect costume would be easy for him to make.

Over the next few days, as Josh worked on the costume, Amy relentlessly practised her jungle song and dance. She moved as if her arms and legs were being pulled by strings. Josh had to acknowledge that she looked just like a lanky stick insect might, if it could dance. The song was catchy, and Josh found himself subconsciously humming along with Amy as he worked.

Josh created the long arms and legs of Amy's stick insect costume from cardboard tubes joined together with brown string. The body was speckled with paint and glued-on leaves. Best of all, Josh was making a pair of stilts for Amy to stand on. The stilts, in Josh's mind, were the magical ingredient that would turn Amy into an awesome stick insect.

Three days before the production started, Josh finished the stilts. Amy strapped them on and got Josh to help her stand up. It took a bit of practice to get her balance, but she was soon wobbling up and down the concrete driveway like a newborn foal.

"Please be careful," said Josh apprehensively, biting his lip. "Walking on stilts takes a lot of practice."

But Amy didn't hear him. She was shouting for her friends next door to come and see. "Look at me," she cried. "I'm so tall!"

Amy was having so much fun that she didn't see the neighbour's little dog run up the driveway. He started yapping in excitement at Amy on the stilts. Taken by surprise, Amy missed a step. Teetering precariously, she tried to get her balance, frantically wheeling her arms in the air like a supercharged turbine. But… it was too late. With a scream, she went crashing onto the concrete.

Everybody came running. Josh's face had gone as white as paper. Amy was screaming like a siren. Somebody called an ambulance. Amy had broken her leg.

Home from hospital, Mum sat Amy on the couch, propping her plastered leg up on cushions. Amy's voice could be heard reverberating through the entire house. "I am *not* going to stay home! I don't need those silly stilts! I can *still* be a stick insect!"

"Amy," explained Mum, "the doctor said you mustn't do anything energetic. You've got to let your leg heal."

Tears sprang into Amy's eyes. "But I *can* do it," she cried. "I *know* I can!"

Mum simply shook her head. No matter how much Amy protested, there was no way she was going to be in the school production now.

Ms Smith, who had written all the songs for the show, came to visit Amy. "It's such a shame," she said. "Nobody else will be able to learn the song and the dance in time."

"Actually," said Dad, "there is somebody who knows the song and the dance back to front. You might say Amy has got an understudy."

Ms Smith looked surprised. "But who would that be?"

Dad clapped a hand on Josh's shoulder.

Realising what Dad was saying, Josh vigorously shook his head.

"Of course," said Mum with a big smile. "Josh could do it."

"No way," whispered Josh. And, before anybody could say anything more, he hurried out of the room.

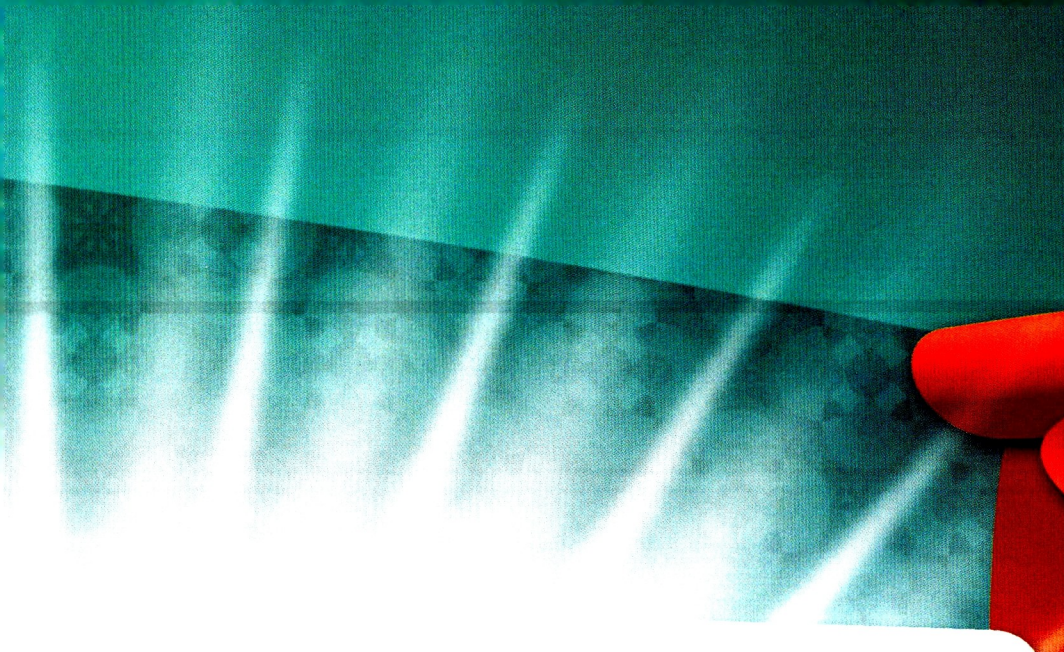

All that afternoon, Josh hid in the garden with a book.
When Dad came out looking for him, Josh hid in the
woodshed. He was not going to go on stage in front of the
whole school. That evening, when Josh had finally come
inside, he and Amy were sitting in the lounge, watching
television. Amy gave her brother a nudge.

"Why don't you want to be the stick insect?" she asked.

"Because," said Josh, "everybody will be staring at me."

"They won't be looking at you," said Amy. "They'll be
looking at a stick insect!"

Josh said nothing. But later that night, before he went
to bed, Josh had a quiet word with Dad.

Two nights later, the family entered the school hall, along with all the rest of the audience. Mum pushed Amy in a wheelchair. She waved at everybody like a queen from her carriage.

Behind the curtains, kids were milling around in excitement. There were tigers and frogs and monkeys and leafy, walking trees. In one dim corner, towering over everybody, stood a tall, brown stick insect. Ms Smith, holding a clipboard, hurried over.

"Are you ready, Josh?"

The stick insect's eyes were huge, but he nodded.

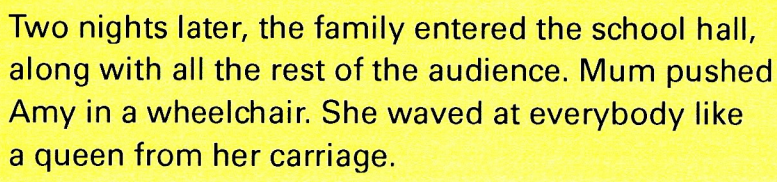

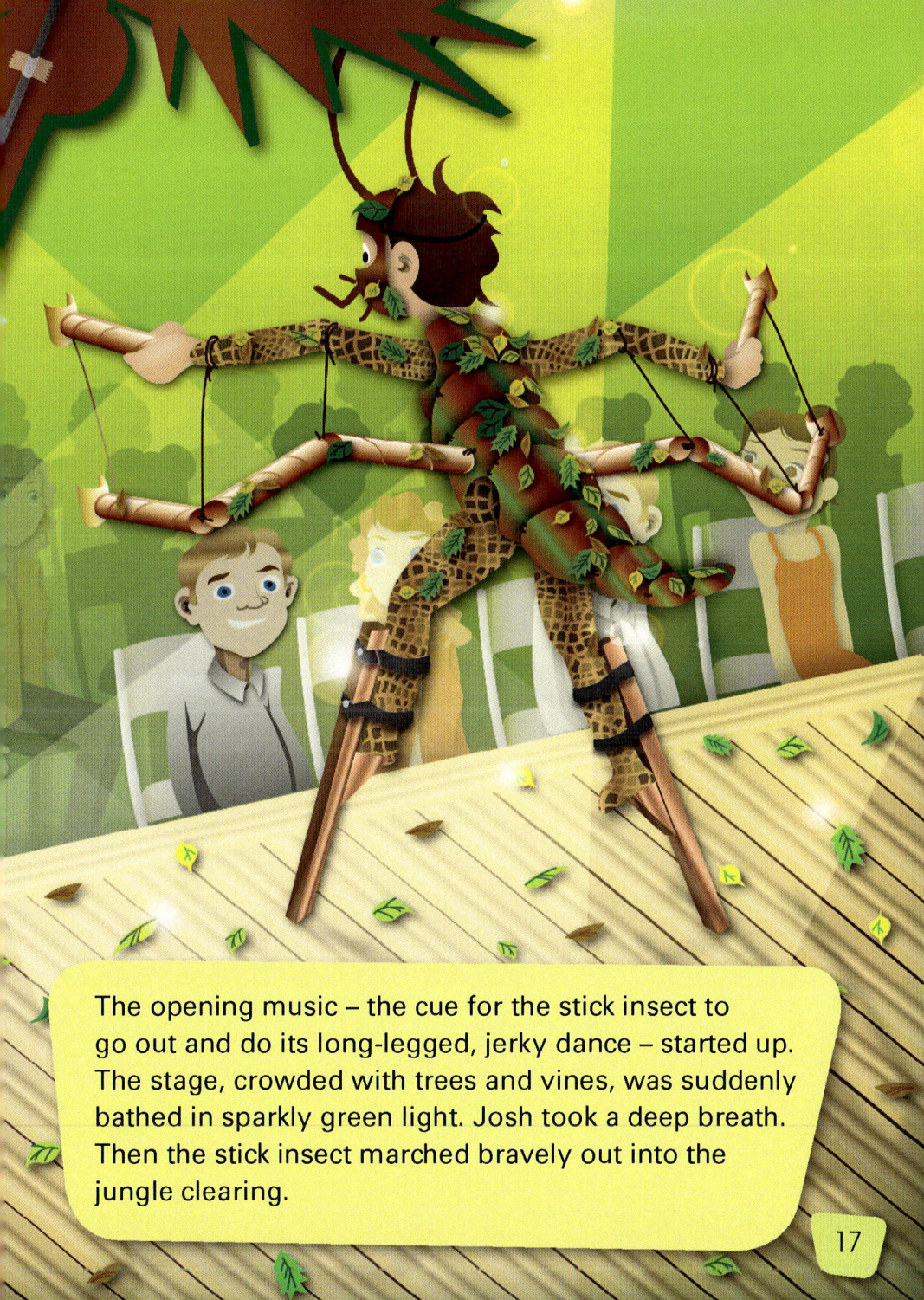

The opening music – the cue for the stick insect to go out and do its long-legged, jerky dance – started up. The stage, crowded with trees and vines, was suddenly bathed in sparkly green light. Josh took a deep breath. Then the stick insect marched bravely out into the jungle clearing.

Narratives

Narratives tell a story. You are the storyteller. You tell the story for the characters about what happened through your eyes as a spectator.

How to Write a Narrative

Step One

Decide on a storyline.
Your storyline should have these things:

An Introduction that quickly tells the readers:

• Who the story is about (the characters).
• Where and when the story happened (the setting).

A Problem

Amy breaks her leg and can't take part in the school production. Her brother Josh could stand in for her, but he doesn't like people looking at him.

A Solution

Amy persuades Josh to take her part. She tells him the audience won't be looking at him – they will be looking at a stick insect.

Remember

The problem creates excitement/interest and makes the reader want to find out how the problem is solved.

Step Two

Think about the main **characters** and describe what they look like and how you imagine they might think, act and feel.

Amy
- eleven-year-old girl
- likes to be centre of attention
- talks and sings at the top of her voice
- exuberant and confident
- likes to show off
- shows determination and persistence

Josh
- ten-year-old boy
- quiet and shy
- doesn't talk much
- good with hands and making things
- supportive and caring
- doesn't like people staring at him
- thinks things through

Step Three

Think about the **setting**.

Where did the events happen?
What might the characters:

 see   hear   feel smell or taste?

Step Four

Think about the **events** in order of sequence.

▬▬ **Guide Notes**

Title: The Stick Insect

Stage: Advanced Fluency

Text Form: Narrative

Approach: Guided Reading

Processes: Thinking Critically, Exploring Language, Processing Information

Written and Visual Focus: Speech Bubbles

THINKING CRITICALLY

(sample questions)

- Look at pages 2–3. What do you think might happen in this story?
- How do you think the author wanted the reader to see Amy? Do you think Amy will be a likeable character from your first impression of her? Why or why not?
- Look at pages 4–5. What inferences can you make about why Josh spent a lot of time working on projects in the garage?
- Look at pages 6–7. What was meant by the term "the song was catchy"?
- What inferences can you make about Josh as a brother?
- Look at pages 8–9. Why do you think Josh's face went white? Do you think he felt responsible for the accident? Why or why not?
- Look at pages 10–11. How do you think the author wanted the reader to feel when she wrote about Amy's efforts to keep her part in the school production?
- Do you think Mum was fair when she stopped Amy from performing in the production? What is your opinion?
- Look at pages 12–13. Do you think it was fair of Mum and Dad to promote Josh for Amy's part in the production? Why or why not?
- Look at pages 14–15. What connections can you make to Josh and his feelings of shyness? If he were a friend, how might you help him?
- What inferences can you make about Amy from her comment to Josh that people would be "looking at a stick insect"?
- Do you think the conclusion to this story works? Why or why not?
- Why do you think the author wrote this story?
- Who would you recommend this story to and why?

EXPLORING LANGUAGE

Vocabulary

Clarify: exuberantly, smugly, complicated, elaborate, project, relentlessly, acknowledge subconsciously, ingredient, apprehensively, teetering precariously, supercharged turbine, reverberating, vigorously, milling around

Synonyms: Discuss synonyms for *relentlessly, acknowledge, apprehensively, protested*

Simile: *like a newborn foal, like a supercharged turbine, like a queen waving from her carriage*